DESPERATION QUOTIENT

IT'S ABOUT THE FIRE IN YOUR BELLY

EXCLUSIVELY FOR SALES PROFESSIONALS

I0504132

ANIL RAO KULKARNI

INDIA · SINGAPORE · MALAYSIA

Notion Press Media Pvt Ltd

No. 50, Chettiyar Agaram Main Road,
Vanagaram, Chennai, Tamil Nadu – 600 095

First Published by Notion Press 2021
Copyright © Anil Rao Kulkarni 2021
All Rights Reserved.

ISBN 978-1-68563-293-9

Contents

Foreword

You are no one until you become someone, and that highly depends on who you work with. I was lucky to have worked with extraordinary professionals from across different countries including India, Singapore, Japan, Germany, Australia, UK & the USA.

I strongly believe that "You become what your manager is". I am saying this from my 20 long years of work experience. You learn so much from your managers, they make a strong influence on your career. In my case, my managers' influence has been 100%. I owe this book, this knowledge and the experience to all my managers and influencers.

I am fortunate to have genuine managers throughout my career. I would like to name those who have contributed significantly in shaping my career. I shall mention them in an order of my career path.

Back in 1998, Satish Joshi was my first manager at Philips, India, taught me to *"stay aligned with your manager."* Atul Bhasin at IBM taught me how to *"pull up your sleeves and make things happen."*

I moved to Singapore in 2001. My boss Joseph KW Chan at Fujitsu Singapore, a soft power, taught me how to *"keep the team motivated and happy."* Late Choi Chee Kong, my super boss at Fujitsu was and is still a benchmark when it comes to the 'Sales Profession'. Choi was extremely charming and a winner. He always had a way to charm anyone around him, be it a customer, a partner, or an employee. I moved back to India in 2007 for good, to further the development Fujitsu business in India.

I met Sanjay Hiranandani in 2005 at a Marketing Event, we hit it off smooth because we had a common agenda. We still have a good relationship. He is still a friend and a guide even after 15 years of association. My success in the sales profession is very much a consequence of working with Choi and Sanjay.

I was my manager for a couple of years until Mikito Kiname showed up as the CEO of Fujitsu India in 2009. Kiname San had a great influence on me, he was calm like an ocean as long as there was no storm. Pallab Talukdar took over from Kiname San. Pallab was a great deal of energy and truly a technocrat, a great storyteller. Then comes Mark Wilson, who once told me *'if you are too polite people will term you as stupid and walk over you'*. This statement changed me completely, for good. After 15 years of my service to Fujitsu, in 2016 I moved to vCentric where I enjoyed working with MVR Kumar, a key takeaway from working with MVR was that the best decisions can't be based on a one-sided story, unless you are a mind reader.

vCentric was acquired by itelligence in 2017, where I met Sanjeev Deshpande. Sanjeev is *truly a visionary, humble and a People Manager.* His ability to listen to others', their ideas and thoughts must have made him a visionary leader that he is. While I am still learning greater things from Sanjeev, I have another manager Christian Brink, I am learning how to be d*ynamic and yet stay focused* on execution.

I must mention Rainer Hettinger, a colleague and a friend who taught me a lesson worth a million dollars '*how to achieve things without politicizing, in a friendly manner*'.

My story will be incomplete without mentioning Darrell van Rensburg, truly an Australian. Darrell, as straight as an arrow, taught me how to keep things simple, how to simplify complex things, it works as a wonder.

All these learnings have turned me into a *Thinker and a story teller.* Hope you like reading about *"Desperation Quotient [DQ]"*, a story that I am presenting to you through this book, while my learning continues…

Namaste!
Anil Rao Kulkarni

Introduction

Human beings are blessed with every possible factors that are required for success and it only differs a little from one individual to another. We all have been blessed with abilities, talents, free will, and the option to choose whether to use them or not. Most certainly every action taken by an individual will require certain levels of choice to be made with respect to the success or failure of the action. The power to decide whether to win or fail lies greatly in our hands and since we are the architect of our actions, we must live with the outcome, whether glorious or tragic. With that being said, there are markers of success and failure, and prominent among the markers is a certain concept called effort. Effort as you may learn about is a conscious exertion of physical or mental power geared towards achieving success in tasks. The efforts put into a task involving all the earnest and conscientious activities intended towards the completion of the task.

While achieving success in tasks and life, in general, may need a lot of efforts, there is the concept of capabilities. Capability is the quality or state of being able to perform some certain things. It is the power of ability to generate a desired outcome from tasks. Capability may be regarded to as the best marker for success and this is because being capable would mean that one is naturally blessed with the skillset and talents to carry out tasks without adding too much hard work or efforts to it. It is becoming quite lucid in differentiating between the two concepts that has been highlighted – Effort and Capability. I know most of us would agree and admit to the fact that some people are more talented than the others in specific areas but yet, we can also quite agree that everyone can work hard to achieve the same ends. The only difference would be the time taken and energy expended which will vary from one individual to the other.

To be very candid there is a very complex relationship between effort and capability. There are two sides to understanding the relationship between the two concepts. On the first side, there is a natural tension between the two concepts, and one concept cannot be mentioned without the other standing somewhere in the picture as an antagonist. The capability would naturally mean that tasks are easier to complete for some and relatively not so easy to carry out for others. Essentially, capability is performance minus effort which signifies that the more capable you are, the less effort you have to put into reaching a certain level of performance or success. So, if you want to outperform other individuals who are more capable than you, it means you would have to work harder and add extra efforts unless there is luck on your side or those individuals choose to be complacent.

On the flip side, we could consider that one is the fuel through which the other one burns. We could say effort is mostly driven by some characteristics and traits which include but are not limited to – ambitiousness, drive, conscientiousness, and focus. In such a case we could classify all these traits as the factors that encapsulate the concept of capability. So on this flip side, we could actually say effort is sometimes driven by capability. Generally speaking, there are two schools of thought about understanding efforts and ability and so we have a dichotomy, and trying to understand the dichotomy is a stressful thing itself. We could argue that the two concepts could be distinct of each other and thus we can understand one without the other and meanwhile it could also be that the two work in a somewhat intermingled and in consequence they are both coordinate rather than exclusive. The most appealing perspective is the latter which is of the position that you cannot speak of any of the concept without possibly mentioning the other one.

If we relate this side of the argument to the business world in general then it would mean that in some organizations, we would likely see staffs that would have capability and would not add so much efforts into tasks because they can actually achieve tasks with less hassles. And more so, in this same organization we would most likely see staffs that are less capable but are willing to put more efforts into tasks to boost productivity. The main of any business entity is to maximize profit while achieving laid-down goals. In order to achieve this, there has to be a balance between capabilities and efforts that go into achieving general and professional goals. This balance is known as the line of desperation. When one is desperate, there is a dire need for result and performance and thus is a shift from depending on capability to depending on efforts exerted into tasks. To achieve success, there has to be moderate desperation that would see capability meet with efforts in order to achieve tasks. The major scope of this book is the marketing/sales sector and we could try to imagine the usefulness of discovering what could help you as a salesperson to hit your best.

Thus, this book is focused on discussing the ratio between the capabilities and the efforts that are involved in achieving personal and professional goals. This ratio is known as the **Desperation Quotient** and the book will bring into limelight the line between being desperate enough and becoming over desperate in achieving the goals. The book will focus more on the Sales and Marketing profession as it would help to analyze the performance indicators of sales personnel as well as guide people in understanding the reasons behind their potential sales success or failures. The book promises a lot and lot of gains and other usefulness as Desperation quotient can be used in many fields and many aspects of an individual's life even up to the extent that you could use it to find the right job or a befitting life partner. Keep on reading, there is a lot to plunder.

Chapter One

Understanding Desperation Quotient

One must have enough desperation, enough fire in the belly to achieve good things in life, be it a personal goal or a professional goal. If you want a bigger house or a faster car you need to go that extra mile, you need to work hard. In addition, you must ensure that the extra mile you are going is in the right direction, which means, the knowledge about getting something done must be acquired, desperation alone is not good enough. It takes months or even years for some people to prepare for an expedition to climb mountains or to run a marathon.

Over desperation, meaning attempting to do things without knowledge of it will destroy your confidence, your time, your health, and your motivation. Try and try until you get success is fine but don't start with it without required preparation, don't have to take unnecessary risks in life, rather acquire required knowledge prior to even your first attempt of getting anything done. You shouldn't even try to make an omelet without knowing how to break an egg, you can save a lot of mess.

Many times, we get lost in an epic battle between success and relaxation. There are times we need relaxation but then our thirst for success gets us up on our feet in the quest of success and there are some times when we ultimately choose rest and relaxation over work. In this case, there is never anyone to blame as both are necessary in a man's life as working without rest would just ensure one drops dead at an early age while all rest with no work will only give unto one a mediocre, less-fulfilling life. However, between work and rest only one is easy to get and that is the latter. It is never a difficult task not wanting to work but then one cannot succeed without having to work. Many people want to succeed in life. In fact, everyone wants to attain a certain level of freedom that would see them fulfill their dreams but sadly, only a few of us are willing to do what it takes to achieve those dreams. For success to be attained, one needs to have a disciplined approach towards work as well as persistence, courage, and the endurance to withstand the pressure that comes with work. However, naturally, there are some characteristics that set some people apart from the rest. Those qualities make some people look more naturally able to perform certain tasks or achieve things with relative ease. It is known as natural abilities or talents and overtime humans have devised a way to measure these talents in order to know the extent to which one possesses it. You might have heard about IQ, EQ, or SQ back then; these are the measurements of natural abilities.

Intelligence Quotient (IQ) is a test with scores that represents a person's intelligence and reasoning ability. Originally formulated by Alfred Binet, the intelligence tests are designed to measure crystallized and fluid intelligence. Crystallized intelligence involves one's acquired knowledge and skills while fluid intelligence encompasses one's natural abilities to reason, solve problems and the ability to make sense out of abstract information. The concept was later conceptualized by psychologist William Stern. Following which, there comes Emotional Intelligence Quotient (EQ), which is the ability to understand, use and manage one's emotions in positive ways to relieve stress, communicate effectively, empathize with others, overcome challenges and defuse conflicts. EQ includes some key skills, in the following times, carries additional subheads viz., self-awareness, which includes emotional awareness, self-evaluation, and self-confidence; self-regulation, which includes self-control, reliability, awareness, adaptability and innovation; and soft skills, including influence, leadership, change management, communication, cooperation ad conflict management. Then there is Social Intelligence Quotient which was postulated by Edward Thorndike, but, later reinvented by Howard Gardner and Daniel Goleman.

SQ, simply speaking, is the capacity to know oneself and to know others. SQ includes multiple intelligence which is categorized into two, i.e., intrapersonal and interpersonal intelligence. The important of the two is interpersonal intelligence, which includes sensitivity to the moods, feelings, temperaments, and motivations of others; and the ability to cooperate within a group. Social Intelligence develops from experiences with people as well as learning from the success and failures in social settings. The aforementioned, that is: IQ, QE, and QS, are essential for the success and well-being of any individual, but they don't necessarily have to define absolute success. People with an often similar IQ, EQ, and SQ end up having varied degrees of success in life and so to really measure one's capacity and desperation for success, there came the *"Desperation Quotient [DQ]."*

Desperation Quotient [DQ] is the ratio between the *capabilities* and the *efforts* that go into achieving personal and professional goals. Desperation Quotient reflects abilities to use intelligence, emotions & experience to take timely actions and make timely decisions. However, it will be interesting to see how one can improve their DQ over a period of time by monitoring their capabilities and efforts required to deliver the desired results. How fast and well you can achieve goals is very dependent on your Desperation Quotient. The more desperate you are, the more you are open to doing what it takes to achieve your set goals. Perhaps one of the major reasons why people do not achieve goals on time is because they do not find the urgency of achieving the goal. Desperation in this context can be likened to a force that propels you to put all skillsets and efforts you have at your disposal towards the achievement and attainment of the set goals. To be successful, you need a compelling goal that wakes you up every morning and prompts you to jump out of bed to take massive actions. This compelling force pushes one to use all the available resources at one's ability to achieve goals and these resources include natural abilities known as talents and acquired abilities through efforts. The Desperation Quotient (DQ) is the measurement of success potentialities by understanding one's ability to merge skills and effort required to achieve personal and professional goals.

In this book, we are going to focus more on the *sales profession*. The profession is a very beautiful one with its own peculiar complexities that arise from meeting people who are the potential customers and partners. Due to the erratic nature of all men or women, a salesperson cannot be sure of the type of humans he/she would meet each new day. There are days when everything would move smoothly, sales would boom up and there is motivation to continue working for oneself and then the next day may be so unfruitful that one gets a dampened morale at the end of the day. On such days, you meet unyielding people who are not easy to convince into buying the services or products that you offer. Days like these take a big toll on one's emotions that it is always difficult to pick oneself up from its ashes and funnily, that challenge in specific cuts across all sales personnel; be it ones with extreme skills or the ones with seemingly endless efforts. We are all humans after all and emotions always have their way around us no matter how tough we may seem. Now in this case, what we will need as a force that combines our efforts and abilities into desperation for success and pushes us to move on from the emotional shackles of failure that ensued from a previous fruitless day.

Desperation Quotient (DQ) is a measurement with 4 probable outcomes: Low, Hyper, Poor and Optimum zones.

Low DQ zone: Individuals who fall under this category have a personality that is low in efforts and capabilities. These are people who have neither the passion nor the skills to excel in their profession. They do not possess the natural skills as well as the hard work factor to execute plans. They are often relegated to the lower echelons of an organization despite many years of work experience.

Hyper DQ Zone:
Individuals under this zone have a high level of effort and relentless hard work but relatively low natural  capabilities and skills needed. As these people display great energy and positivity, they are often mistaken for great performers at first. However, their innate incompetence manifests itself very quickly and can lead to great disappointment for their employers.

 ***Poor DQ Zone:*** Can be described as "lazy": These people have great intelligence and great ability. But the lack of effort that accompanies a lack of ambition leads to poor DQ. Over time, they can become irritating in an organization, especially if they cannot accept the professional growth of their peers. Organizations would do well to identify these people at an early stage and remove them from the system.

Optimum DQ: They are the leaders and the winners in the truest sense of the word. The quality that is evident in all people in the Optimum DQ zone is their thirst for success. Ambition, the desire to excel, pushes them. For them, knowledge is essential, and they will constantly  try to update their knowledge and skills.

It is now quite apparent the role of effort and capabilities in the life of an individual. Both work interdependently to make one be at Optimum rate of one's game. There is a need to know how to blend both to one's advantage because unless this is done, it is almost earthly impossible to get to the Optimum stage. No matter your skill level or productivity level, there is always a window to do a better job than what has been done in the past. Watching one's skills, improving them it and exploring ways to learn something new is one of the steps to becoming a better version of yourself. Not only does this help improve your professional performance, it also creates potential opportunities for your career development.

How to achieve the best in Sales Profession?

With the importance of constant and never-ending personal improvement in mind, I have put together some work management tips that are sure to improve your effort and capabilities and they are being discussed below:

At a high level, I strongly believe that if you are disciplined and hardworking, you can get to wherever you want to, you will become unstoppable. Let me elaborate a little more on what these two characteristics mean for Sales Professionals.

Like every other profession sales profession also calls for strict discipline. If you are not disciplined enough you can't deliver consistent results. Many people think that the sales profession is cool, you can do whatever and whenever, which is completely wrong. You have to be disciplined about grooming yourself and your team, you have to be disciplined about acquiring knowledge and skills, and you have to be disciplined about engaging the customers and partners pleasantly. If you follow the discipline half your job is done.

Hard work is the only shortcut to success. If you want to reach that success faster, you need to ensure you are on the right track. Before you start running with the sales numbers, you need to know the directions in which you can achieve your sales goals faster. If you are not clear about this part, you will start losing your confidence after you have lost few deals. However, if you have a thought-through plan, you will know that you are losing the battles but you are prepared to win the war. If you don't have a plan, you may get tired and agitated, which is not good for the sales professional. When you prepare well, you will look confident and cool, smart.

What is now left is in the execution, like they say 'the devil is the details,' here we go...

Setting clear milestones:

Setting clear goals is important in personal and professional life. As humans, we are used to shooting at the stars, and this is reflected in the goals we set for ourselves. It's okay to be a little bold, but when it comes to "goals," it's best to think clearly and be realistic.

Setting goals can be a difficult task. So, break down your big personal and professional plans into smaller parts and set your goals accordingly. It will help you stay motivated and keep your Optimum DQ throughout the journey. Plus, setting clear goals will make it easier for you to track your progress. Allowing you to celebrate every little victory you win. When setting milestones, keep the following tips in mind:

- Make sure you understand the strengths and weaknesses of your company and what you want to sell.

- Make sure you know your competition, your focus on the industries and the technologies.

- Make sure you know what customer problems your company can solve, what you can add as real value to your customer. Build a good story, you have to believe in it 100%.

- Break down your sales targets and demand generation targets into smaller and linear numbers, it will be less stressful and more fun as you achieve those numbers. Do not wait for a big deal to happen to achieve your targets. Big deals must be treated like a 'Blue Bird'.

- Spending more time with your customers and partners is the key, build a stronger yet professional relationship with your customers and partners.

Plan and prioritize

If you think you've heard this point before, you're right. Organizing, planning, and setting priorities are an integral part of our daily routine. Here are some simple work habits and time management tips to help you get things done on time and improve your overall performance at work.

Before you start the day, review the list of tasks or activities you have planned for the day. Now use a planning tool to set a due date and priority status for each task. After that, consider the most urgent and essential tasks and get them done as soon as possible. These are some tips that can help you along the way:

- Understand the difference between "urgent" and "important." Always focus on activities that require immediate attention.

- Try to sort your activities by estimated effort.

- Uncertainty is a reality. So be flexible and adaptable, but keep priorities in mind.

Plan your meetings well

Meetings have a lot of influence, but they're often misunderstood. Planning and scheduling a meeting is a standard procedure in nearly every workplace. This is why it is important to carefully plan each meeting to make it "the most effective."

Take the time to plan your meetings, but keep it short. Make sure all the necessary items are in place before the meeting begins. Set a clear meeting time and communicate it to all participants so that they are better prepared. In addition,

- Before sending out meeting invitations, ask yourself if it's really necessary.

- Check everyone's availability and choose the ideal time for the meeting.

- Provide as many details as possible for preliminary preparation.

- Record a deadline for the meeting and summarize it within the specified deadline.

Communicate Better

Communication is a two-way road. Effective communication is a practice that gives you confidence in things at work, learns new and better ways to achieve better results, and ultimately improves overall performance at work. Remember that every opinion is important and can definitely help you improve your effort and capability.

Consider incorporating an application or a powerful team communication tool in your workflow. Evaluate the different options available in the market, including group messaging apps, discussion boards, and group chat apps, video conferencing tools, and more. Identify the tool or software that would be best for your team, and then use it to collaborate successfully in the workplace. And while doing so, keep the following points in mind:

- Don't just evaluate the available option; put in place a suitable collaboration strategy first.
- Determine which tool will meet your long-term business needs.
- Analyze feedback from customers who have already used your preferred tool.

Conquer difficult tasks first

This point is directly related to our previous point of "plan and prioritize." Of course, you can't do all the tasks or activities at the same time. This is why it is important to understand which tasks need to be accomplished first and which tasks can be postponed or delegated during the planning phase of the project.

Try to prioritize and categorize each item on your to-do list based on its relevance and urgency. Start reviewing the list items from top to bottom, keeping the "most important tasks" at the top. This trick is very straightforward: if an activity seems a little complicated to you, relax your mind by getting rid of it as soon as possible.

Stay focused *(eliminate interruptions)*

Workplace interruptions and distractions can be in all shapes and sizes. It does not matter how many times you've been interrupted during the day or who interrupts you the most. What matters is how you avoid work interruptions and improve your performance. Remember that work interruption is dangerous. You are prompt to lose focus, waste time, and ultimately stop managing your work and delay projects.

If you want to work without interruptions or disruptions, you need to stay away from the phone or email. Turn off the notification and monitor the success of the tasks in question. Also, learn to say "no" if necessary. You can and should say no to anything that could interrupt your day. Beyond that, here are some simple habits to help you stay focused:

- Turn off distractions during working hours. (smartphones, social media sites, office chats, etc.)

- Take short breaks between work and listen to your favorite song or take a short walk.

Recognize your strengths and weaknesses

The phrase "perfect" is too good to be true. There is no way you can be perfect in everything. We all have weaknesses, and it is important to recognize them identify the opportunities for improvement. In addition, each individual has his own strength, that for which he is exceptionally talented. Now, to improve your daily work performance, you need to both love your strengths and overcome your weaknesses.

Never settle for *good* enough when you can be *awesome*. Be your own critic and constantly assess your performance for possible improvements. If you are good enough at something, do all it takes to be the best. Wondering how to understand your strengths and weaknesses? Here are some ideas you can try:

- Find patterns in your performance.

- Decide what you prefer at work.

- Practice Reflective Best Self Exercises (RBS) - Find Out What Others Think About You.

- Note how you react to situations that require action, thought, and intuition.

Be aware of your limits

While it's important to actively seek out ways to improve in the places where you're lacking, it's also important to be aware of your limitations. Never fall victim to habits such as procrastination or multitasking. Act on one task at a time and do your best to make it less stressful and less prone to mistakes or rework. Keep it clear in your mind and you can accomplish a lot more than you planned on, a lot faster.

Understanding your limits is not easy. In reality, you won't be able to comprehend them until you overcome them. Simply put, you need to draw a line between being productive at work and being stressed out at work. And how will you do this? Well, here are some things you can try:

- Learn to say "no" politely and keep the peace.
- Walk away when the going gets tough.
- Don't be too ambitious, be realistic.
- Discover your sweet spot and avoid burnout.

Finish what you start

Another thing that could affect efforts and capabilities at work is leaving things unfinished. Do you remember how many times you started working on something and stopped shortly after? If this happens frequently, it's time for a change. Don't make a habit of leaving things in the middle. If you have started a project or a business, make sure it reaches the final stage with the highest quality.

Set rewards for yourself. Make a habit of celebrating success and rewarding yourself every time you succeed in a project or activity. This way, your performance at work will increase, and you will always have something to look forward to at work.

Use the right tools

Keep you and the team up-to-date with the latest tools and technologies. Presentations, Emails and CRM tools are a must for the sales job. Most of the corporates however small or big they are providing these tools to their teams. If you are part of start-up and these tools are not available to you, you must explore SaaS based tools at the minimum. Without these tools it's nearly impossible to execute sales.

Explore the multitude of options available in the market and evaluate the best one based on your specific business needs.

We have come to the end of this segment of this book that made sure that readers are made to understand the meaning of the concept of the Desperation quotient. The segment went further to enlighten the readers on the necessity of efforts and capabilities in the life of an individual. The segment ends with pro tips on how to improve efforts and capabilities, while ensuring to get work and tasks done. The next segment of this book would see it discuss the first technical aspect of the concept being discussed – Desperation Quotient. The next segment brings to the fore the Desperation Quotient graph that illustrates the aforementioned four zones of Desperation Quotient while linking it to the probabilities of outcomes in the sales profession that is our focal subject matter. See you in the next page.

Chapter Two

Desperation Quotient Graph

In the previous section of this book, readers were presented with 4 zones of Desperation Quotient and were briefed on the general characteristics of the 4 zones. This aspect of the book is crafted to give a graphical representation of those 4 zones in relation to how much skills and efforts is being put to play. These 4 zones are greatly influenced by in-born skills and capacities of each individual and how much the individual is willing to work hard is known as effort. To do justice to the section, this chapter will set off by presenting four different story-like cases to use as case study. These cases will further make a good reference point and a point of explanation for the likely situations of each zone occupants. Furthermore, it should be noted that the chapter will be premised much on Sales and Marketing profession as already indicated at the start of the book.

Case P:

We are assessing the lifestyle of a certain Mr. P. Growing up, everyone knew the young P had it all in him to be the greatest person in whatever career he laid his hands upon. From a very tender age, he had proven to be somewhat of a mini "Jack of all trades" as he literally had lots of talents and abilities that scope over various fields. He was a skilled athlete, a mesmerizing speaker, a trickster that could move people with words, a sonorous singer, and his academic brilliance could not be overlooked. However, upon growing up, this seemingly "Jack of all trades" became "a master at none." Where did it go wrong?

Let it not be said that he stopped having the skills and abilities he possessed as a teenager. In fact, they are all still there intact and you would occasionally see sparks of greatness within, but, the major problem is that there is no notable effort towards maximizing the skills and abilities. It could be that the plethora of abilities get to his head a lot or it could be that he over trusts his abilities to fit into plenty places, only one thing is certain – he does not put efforts into getting the full potentials of his abilities. There is abundance of dormant skills waiting to be activated but there is a doubt there sleeping talents would wake up. Mr. P knows for sure that he is an embodiment of abilities and he takes pride in that fact.

About 6 months ago, Mr. P landed at a dream job with a very big organization as a sales representative and product developer. The employers were glad to add such a huge talent to the workforce and there was an instantaneous effect of the young man's abilities in the marketing department. Everyone knew something different had entered into the fray and for about 3 months there was upraise in the sales taskforce of the organization. The first three months were a success but then the marketing talents and abilities had been utilized and by the middle of the fourth month, things were starting to return to ordinary. 3 months of prosperity had seen people get used to a norm set by Mr. P himself and so it had gotten to a point when Mr. P needed to give more than what he had established as a norm. At this point, he could not deliver something new and innovative. He could only bask in his past achievement. The abilities were there, but no efforts to exploit the abilities and turn them into new innovations. His productivity was under scrutiny now.

It's the sixth month now since P got the job and it is sad to say that there is no longer any marked difference that P has contributed to the development of the organization. In the sales department, his prominence had been overtaken by other peers who have overtime added efforts into bringing solutions and innovation into the organization. Luckily for him, there are few people in his place of work that were able to identify his problems and they were able to advise him to exploit new ways of creating innovations. He knows now that creating innovations cannot be done from his comfort zone so he has to add more efforts. That's his way out.

Case H:

Case H brings into existence a certain lady that would be named as H. H happens to be a very hardworking fellow who would devote time and energy into achieving her aims. From childhood, she was not a very exceptionally skilled kid, but by the virtue of her hard work she was able to close to the level of some of her best friends and colleagues. H could do anything to achieve her aims even though she does not have the knowledge of some technical aspects. She was able to finish college with good grades thanks to hard work and was also able to land a job as a salesperson due to her display of vigor and determination to get work done which in contemporary times, is difficult to get.

Her hard work and efforts makes it very easy to get customer and she could also wait and work for as long as it would take to convince customers. However, something was lacking – the technical know-how of the business. She had the strength but not the in-depth knowledge of what the job entails and consequentially her returns were not really great. She was working quite hard and everyone could see it but the yields of the efforts are often too meagre in the actual sense of everything. However, due to her determination, she is thus being placed on some strategic studies of the work by her employers to give her a technical edge along with her boundless efforts – a reward for her strong character and tenacity. Moral here is that regardless of inabilities, hard work pays.

Case A:

There is Mr. A, the only son of a rich business mogul and a very reputable business woman. While growing up, A had been influence by everyone around him wrongly. He had been told from a young age that even though he does not work, he would still get the finest things of life. This was made real to him. As a student, he had the finest things even though he wasn't doing particularly well in his studies. He never demanded anything without getting it. And he doesn't even put in any efforts at all. Due to all these, it is very difficult to know if A has any talents at all. He doesn't seem to be good at anything. He has no skills per say and he is not the type to devote time and effort into discovering any inherent skills. He is just not the type ready to stress himself and he knows quite clearly he won't need to. He was born with life already set for him.

He managed to finish high school and college. It was time for him to get a job and as always it wasn't a hard task due to his parents' influences locally and internationally. With premium connections, he was able to land a top job being a senior sales department officer. As a salesperson, A had no abilities neither does he the effort to want to learn or make customers want to declare interest and in no time at all everyone knew about A's pure incompetence as it was easily identifiable. He made no major contributions to the company's sales and customers he handled were to have follow-ups raised complaints and got disinterested in the company's products. That way, his lack of skills and laziness couldn't make new customers and could not make him keep the old ones. By his sixth month, he had dealt the sales department so much blow and his employers were looking for how to give him a proper riddance. This was however difficult because of his mode of entry into the job and that was a proper "connection" between A's parents and the owner of the company.

After so many deliberations and meetings, A was to be moved to another department and be giving a non-significant role for the same pay he was being paid – a small price to be paid for the salvation of the sales department. He was never fit for the role of a salesperson and could only excel in a place where his only job was to do nothing. That is definitely what a life without skills and effort looks like. With no promotion ever in sight, he could one day be laid off. Since he has been working ineffectively at the lower echelons of the company, he will remain constant unless he is ready to put some effort into being a better person generally and particularly.

Case D:

The lifestyle of Mr. D is about to be assessed. Mr. D is a man born with great intelligence and ability. He bagged so many awards during his youthful days, he led so many symposiums. While growing up, Mr. D remained intelligent, he continued to excel in whatever career he chose to be in, he was a true example of a leader wherever he found himself. You can bet he won all the scholarship companies had to offer, he seized every opportunity that came his way, and was therefore, very successful. He loved to acquire more knowledge wherever he went, he learnt virtually from anybody; name it, children, schoolteachers, managers, and anybody.

He had this unquenchable thirst for knowledge, which made his colleagues envy him. He had limitless tenacity and energy that exerts to every aspect of his life. He never got tired of leading and winning. Mr. D secured a big job, of course, due to his intelligence and brilliance, as the head of the sales department, in a big company, paying pretty well. The sales department really grew big under his influence, and what was so surprising and good was that, Mr. D really carried everybody in his department along. While he grew, they also grew. He happily shared knowledge and was always ready to help anybody. He was so charismatic and inspiring to work with. Bad days were inevitable in the sales department, but there was a way Mr. D handled bad days and low sales, that is just so comforting and optimistic, so on bad days, he was a good leader, on good days, he was a better leader.

The leaders of his company kept observing these good qualities in him, and when the space for a higher post became vacant, it was only right and just that they let Mr. D fill the vacant position. He got promoted in the space of working for just 8 months in the sales department, something that does not normally happen in the company. People said he was favored, some said he was helped to the position, some said he didn't deserve it, but everybody knew deep down in their hearts, that Mr.

D is an exceptional, intelligent, and born leader. He filled this post, and led his team to success, almost every time, and guess what? He was promoted again, but this time to the Chief Executive Officer of the whole company and beyond. His life was changed totally.

His love for success continued to wax stronger, and he continued to lead the company to good places. There was a clear difference in the way the company was run before, compared to when Mr. D joined. The difference was so plain and crystal clear, that he became a member of the leader's board. He just kept getting promotions, at all ends. He didn't end his career by just sitting on his chair and overseeing affairs, he continued in his quest for knowledge, entering all departments, to offer solutions to their problems, and to give them advice for better productivity.

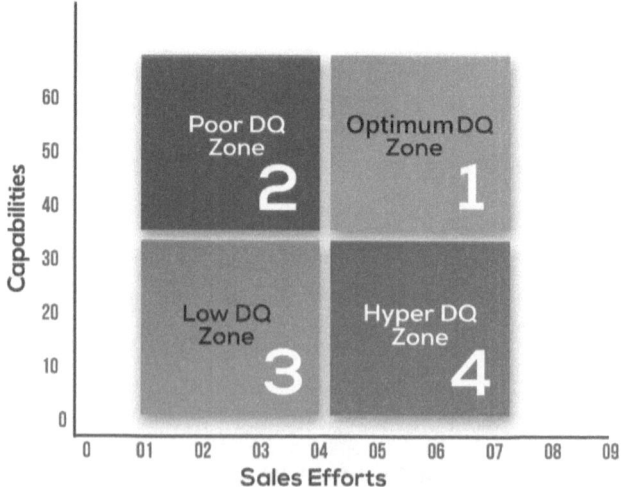

The DQ diagram/graph has four areas as displayed above and these areas demonstrate a person's Desperation Quotient as a function of the provider's efforts and their *ability* to deliver the results. Salesperson skills are measured on the basis of facts such as education and experience, job skills, sales skills, and cross-functional skills. The seller's "sales efforts" are measured by facts such as the number of customers managed, the number of hours a salesperson spends with their customer in a day, the number of customers whom he meets in a week, the number of leads generated, and Sales pipe generated versus the sales targets. This applies to everything from a single track that you want to earn for the long-term goals, which you want to achieve in your career. Now it is imperative to proceed to the graph's explanation with references to the fictional cases presented at the beginning of the chapter.

Poor DQ Zone (High Capabilities, Low – medium Sales efforts):

This is a zone characterized by people or salespersons with abilities to understand how to properly position solutions or services against the market competitors and knows how to fulfil customer needs in the favour of his/her employers. More so, these people may have other non-technical skills related to customer relations and how to get the job done. However, these set of people do not put in enough effort to achieve their sales aim. These people often tend to start off with bright sparks but in the long run, they often turn out to be mediocre. They are tagged as "Lazy" and so they falter in doing the necessary follow up on customers, some may even not have the tenacity of spending enough time with their clients knowing fully well that it takes time to convince some customers on why they should choose one's offer over other market competitors.

In relation to the fictional cases at the start of this chapter, it is quite clear that this zone is similar to that of Case P which portrays a man with high skills and capabilities but with a very meagre level of efforts. Individuals, under this zone, often start well in life generally and career specifically but they burn out of brilliance later as there isn't much effort exerted into other places where only skills won't be enough for them.

Hyper DQ Zone (Low - Medium Capabilities, High Sales efforts):

This zone is the direct opposite to the poor DQ zone and it is mainly characterized with people who have low skills and abilities but are blessed with high efforts and energy. There is abundance of energy which propels individual under this category to work very hard but then there are no existing bundles of talent and job skills. Drawing insights from the Case H in the fictional section, one would see that salesperson in this zone works hard but lacks the basics. The individuals in this zone often press the customers to do business with them, they are good with follow-ups, great in going lengths to find customers.

However such sales persons may come short in areas such as strategy, customer handling, customer management and customer satisfaction.

This means that the sellers in this zone may likely not deliver anything and might ultimately lose against the competition since the customer is not convinced of the solution/service that the seller has placed here. They also pick loss-making deals after lots of efforts being exerted into the customers, they definitely would want to have something to show for it and as such strike less profitable sales deals with customers for their employers.

Low DQ Zone (Low Capabilities, Low Sales efforts):

Individuals, under this zone, always end up failing. There is not much that can be given to an individual with no skills and no efforts. These sorts of persons cannot or should not be given roles of sales personnel as they will not be able to make any difference. Case A shows us that people as such can only get jobs based on *connections* as they are originally not qualified enough for tasks and demanding jobs.

Optimum DQ Zone (High Capabilities, Moderate – High Sales efforts):

This is by far the best DQ Zone and you could already know it is the direct opposite of the Low DQ zone. Individuals under the zone have all potentials and propensities to achieve every of their single life's aspirations. These people will usually achieve their goals because they are fully equipped with knowledge about their business, products, services, culture, and support systems. This knowledge transfers into the seller's confidence when he enters into negotiations with his clients or simply by building a relationship between the client and his organization.

The supplier in the ODQ zone devotes sufficient time and effort to the client organizations. Customers often appreciate this attitude, and customers often prefer this sales team. The customers feel comfortable with the sales staff that works closely with them throughout the sales cycle. An insightful look into Case D in the fictional cases shows us that these people combine their capabilities with efforts to become the best version of themselves on their jobs.

To round off this chapter, it is safe to say readers can easily pick out the best zone of the Desperation Quotient already and that is the Optimum DQ zone. That is not to say people who belong to the other DQ zones cannot improve. There is always room for improvement and that is underlined in the fact of effort-making. However one has to be very balanced so as to avoid hyper, low, and poor DQ zone. This signals the end of this chapter and the next chapter discusses a very important thing and it is about the guidelines to accessing the Optimum DQ zone as a salesperson.

Chapter Three

Guidelines for Accessing ODQ

It's all about the **fire in the belly,** besides the knowledge, job skills, soft skills, your IQ, your EQ, etc. If you don't have the desire to achieve more every day in your life there is no way you will ever enter the Optimum DQ Zone. Following are a few guidelines to enable you to enter this zone and stay there.

Know your job:

Most of the sales guys don't understand what is to deliver. The only thing that your organization is expecting from you is to deliver the sales numbers without hurting the brand and compliance, although it's actually very simple. *What to sell, to whom, how much to sell, and by when.* There are many occasions where the pressure to deliver forces salespeople to do what they are not asked. Some, out of pressure to impress would make sales but in the long, lose customers. So it's best to keep things simple and non-complicated.

Accept what is possible:

Learn to say no, most of the companies expect you to deliver the mountains, but can you? Is the sales target assigned to you unrealistic? How do you know it's unrealistic? It all depends on which position you are in, which country or region you are managing, what portfolio you are carrying? Are you into volume or value business? Your competition etc.

These are questions you should try to answer before committing yourself to the job. If you do not take time to ask yourself all these, you might find yourself falling out tired in a short time. However, you should have a decent sales number that allows companies to make some money beyond absorbing your costs to the company.

Know your market:

Based on the sales numbers and portfolio, you must map it with the market segments, geographies, industries, etc. If you are able to do this you have already achieved a significant milestone. Typically, sales folks start running without understanding the map, you know what happens when you are in unknown territory without a GPS. Take your time and make sure you have mapped your market with your targets.

Knowledge is your best weapon:

If you don't have enough knowledge about your products, the problems they can solve, best suitable industries for your portfolio therefore the best target customers then you are once again running directionless. One must take time to prepare for the market. You must try to become knowledge partner for your customers, earn their respect. When you achieve this, you will be the first person they will connect with when they want to solve some problems in their organization. Your customers don't buy things for the heck of buying, you must remember this.

Therefore, it's very critical to know what values your company, your products, and your people can deliver to your customers both in short term and long term.

It's better to be bought than to be sold:

Don't engage with your customers only to push them to buy, with all honesty, you must engage in a consultative selling. Meaning, expose your customer to all possible solutions and help them chose the best. Don't always make time bound offers, walk the journey with your customers. Remember selling is only the first step into building that beautiful relationship with your customer. Be an advisor to your customer, not a salesman.

Use a 60/20/20 approach to time management:

Rather than spending 100% of your time knocking out tasks using the *Whack-a-Mole* method, I suggest a strategic approach to time management. First, use 60% of your time to proactively focus on activities that really add value to your business or cannot be done by others. The other 40% of your time should be divided into two categories: 20% planning and 20% strategy. Planning is about dedicating time to resources and programs for the operation of the business; Strategy is the time to think about how to improve business performance, the customer experience, or the profit model.

Develop relationships with your customers:

There is nothing like a salesperson without the customers. Create a healthy customer relationship with your customers. Even after your current transactions are complete, make sure to keep in contact with those customers as you don not necessarily have to end relationships with them. Past customers can be an excellent source of new transactions for many years to follow. They could even link you up with new customers and that would not be a bad idea at all.

Persistence with leads ad active follow ups:

Most salespeople, in recent times, are always too concerned with selling immediately and so tend to put aside the habit of following up with leads. They silently give up on customers that do not yield up the first time and try looking elsewhere for new customers. That is very wrong and that displays lack of efforts. According to new researches on sales, a large percentage of sales transactions do not happen on first meeting and it takes an average number of 5 interactions after first contact with a customer before the transaction is wrapped up successfully. If you want to be a savvy salesperson, you must understand the fact that viable leads are to be nurtured until it yields a positive outcome. Send mails, make calls and keep in touch always. That way the customer will always think of you first when they decide to take actions.

Introduce to customer their unconsidered needs:

Being a savvy salesperson means you must have to try out innovative new approaches towards sales. Now one major thing to note is that you should not only base your approach on what your prospective customers tell you that they need. The problem is that your competitors are doing exactly the same thing and so you end up being generic and indifferent. Customers will see no compelling contrasts and thus are made to choose blindly. The solution to this is to introduce to these potential customers the concept of unconsidered needs – that is, unknown problems that they may have because they have not bought the services or products that you represent. Enlighten them on the downside of not purchasing those services on time. That way you are marketing through another approach. You won't just be a tape-recorder playing unto the customers' ears what they have most likely heard several times from competitors.

Be polite when discussing competitors:

You have to put your professionalism in play at all times. There are ways you can present yourself and the brand you represent in positive light without the use of derogatory terms or abusive, foul language when discussing other people's businesses and in the case that the customers start the negative conversation about the competitors, it is best to stay neutral. That is professionalism.

Give yourself the upper hand in price bargain:

We are at the time when customers know they have the power of negotiation in hand. They now approach negotiations with the confidence to demand price cuts, discounts and even walk away once they do not feel okay with the negotiation processes. In old times, salespeople would normally skyrocket the prices so that when the bargains start they would now give a discount that would invariably still amount to the original price they had in mind but times have changed and perspectives have been shifted.

Now as a savvy salesperson, what you need to do is to reframe your buyers' perception about the products you are selling. In one of the aforementioned point, there is one where you introduce to your customers their unconsidered needs. You would need that as well as creative ways to make your products appear as bigger than customers' problems. This approach will create price uncertainty in the customers' minds as they would have had the perceived value of your products disrupted. You increase your value in their mind that the price now looks like okay and bargaining looks irrelevant.

This chapter has mainly discussed one thing – accessing the Optimum DQ of a salesperson. This chapter has highlighted many pro tips that would prove useful to salespeople. The chapter is inspired and written from years of experience as a Sales Executive. The next chapter looks to discuss a more interesting topic – DQ measurement. There has to be a way to measure the level of one's DQ. That is the only way to be able to identify good or bad DQ. The next page is just a page-flip away and so with high hopes, the book expects the readers on the next page. Happy reading!

Chapter Four

DQ Measurement

Up till this very point, this book has covered different aspects and has done justice to the conceptual clarification and an explanatory graph of the zones of Desperation Quotient. The next best thing to do is to have a discourse on how to measure Desperation Quotient. Every human capacity quotient has its own measurement. Without measurement, it is almost impossible to know the actual capacity of a person. Take for instance the Intelligence Quotient (IQ), for one to be able to know the extent of one's IQ, one has to be put under standardized tests or subtests as a way to assess one's intelligence. Other human capacity quotients have their own mode of measurements as well and so, most definitely, there has to be a mode of measurement for Desperation Quotient as well. That is what this chapter sets out to achieve. This chapter has been segmented into two categories – the first of which talks about the general DQ measurement and the second part is streamlined to the measurement of a salesperson's DQ.

General DQ Measurement:

When discussing this, the general measurement of Desperation Quotient, the first thing that would be put into consideration is the general determinants of desperation – Effort and Capabilities. To be able to tell if one has a low or high DQ, the first and major thing to check is the level of skills possessed and the extent to which an individual is willing to work hard in order to reach the optimum level of abilities or to learn that in which the individual does not already know.

Furthermore, putting life's generalities into perspective, one's DQ can be very low if one does not understand one's life goals and no one has asked or cared for too long. DQ can be very high when you've slept too much and wake up to reach your goal. Your DQ can also be very high when you accept a role or extremely challenging goals. One's DQ can be low if there is no internal or external drive or motivation towards the attainment of one's life aspirations or goals. It is that simple to measure.

Salesperson's DQ Measurement:

S N	DQ Parameters	Score (1 - 10 max)	Wtg (1-10 max)	DQA Score Wtg x Score
1	Education & Experience	2		0
2	Job Skills			0
3	Sales Skills	4		0
4	Soft Skills			0
5	Sales Efforts	2		0

This is a high-level guideline, a measurement that can be further enhanced by Human Resource department or the Sales Managers to analyze the sales teams.

In explaining the table above, one has to note that each DQ parameter carries maximum 10 point scores and max., 10 points weightage. More the DQA score better the DQ, is the logic. The weightage for the *Sales Capabilities* and the weightage for *Sales Efforts* are same 10 points. Therefore highest score in both the areas undoubtedly deliver better sales results.

This is a very important aspect of this book. It could be of help to both employers and employees. The sales department of any organization can be likened to the most important department as that department almost single-handedly ensures the company's sales. Therefore, organizations have a vested interest in giving their sales team reasonable goals or ensuring that they are prepared for unpleasant surprises, which is why understanding the measurement of a typical salesperson's DQ is very necessary. DQ of a salesperson is measured based on two categories that span over 5 key parameters. As displayed in the table above, you could see there are two broad categories – *Sales Capabilities* and *Sales Efforts* and the two categories produce a total of 5 key parameters that makes up a salesperson's DQ. The parameters are:

i. Education and Experience

ii. Job skills

iii. Sales skills

iv. Soft Skills

v. Sales Effort

Measuring other Sales Capacity:

To measure sales capacity there are 4 parameters involved and they would be assessed below.

Education and Experience: This is a pivotal aspect of sales capacity. Education in this sense encompasses all the educational backgrounds and the various levels of academics that the any salesperson has made it through. Education goes a long way in shaping the capacity of a salesperson. Let's take for an instance, someone that studied clinical science takes up the role of a salesperson. No matter how hard the person may try to learn, there will still be a visible lack of expertise compared to someone that studied marketing. Educational background surely plays a huge role in sales capacity development. Experience, on the other hand, is the number of years an individual has spent on a particular job. This is also one major area that is used to measure sales capacity which in turn, determines the Desperation Quotient of a salesperson. In contemporary times, experience has become a major determinant of employment. You'd always find companies requesting for a certain number of experience years as a prerequisite for getting a job.

Job Skills: Skills are the expertise or talent needed in order to do a job or task. Job skills, in this sense, allow you to do a particular job effectively and efficiently. There are many different job skills that can help one to succeed at all aspects of one's career. Also known as work skills, Job skills are competences you need to perform tasks a job requires and few general examples include: commercial awareness, business acumen, teamwork, communication, negotiation and persuasion, problem solving skills, leadership, organization, perseverance and motivation. These general abilities would allow most workers to do particularly well in almost all aspects or department in any organization.

Sales Skills: These are characteristics and competencies sales representatives depend on to support customers in making purchases and resolving issues. They are the key abilities that equip sales professionals to successfully communicate with customers and potential customers. These skills include the following: strong communication, prospecting, Business acumen, social selling, active listening, and objection handling and presentation skills amongst the rest.

Soft Skills: Soft skills are character traits and interpersonal skills that characterize a person's relationships with other people. They are non-technical skills that relate to how one works in relation to interaction with colleagues, problem-solving and work stress management. Mostly there are 7 important soft skills to have in any workplace. They are communication, teamwork, adaptability, problem-solving, leadership, work ethics, and time management.

Measuring Sales efforts:

The major way to measure sales effort is through Sale Key Performance Indicators. KPI is a measurable value that demonstrates how effectively a company or departments under a company are achieving the key business objectives. They are critical key indicators of progress toward an intended result. Mainly there are 4 Sales Key Performance Indicators and they are:

   i. Sales Productivity

   ii. Lead Response time

   iii. Opportunity Win Rate

   iv. Average Deal Size

However, there could be various other parameters that might have impact on the sales performance and are common for yourself and your competitions then you have to live with them. Example, the share market crashed and that pushed your customers out of comfort zone and now the customer doesn't want to make investments.

Sales Productivity: This is a measurement of how much time spent by sales representatives while selling. Sales productivity is a key for the management to understand time spent selling helps measure sales performance in terms of efficiency. According to a report from the Sibson Consulting Productivity study, average performing salespersons spend only 35 percent of their time in direct selling while on the other hand, high performing sales reps devote 65 percent of their time selling and the remaining 35 percent in non-sales activities.

Lead Response time: Time is a very valuable thing to put into consideration when calculating sales performance. Like the first point, this one is also about time and it is the amount of time spent on follow ups on leads by sales reps. In this case, the longer the lead response time, the worse the salesperson's performance is.

Opportunity win rate: Before closing a deal, an opportunity must first be created from potential customers. Not every leads met would later be interested in making a customer out of them. Hence, win rate is the measure of how many of those potential customers did you turn into actual customers. As a norm, if the win rate is low, then you know the salesperson is underperforming and vice versa. Also, if the win rate is found to be low or declining, questions may arise as to why there is such. Could it be a loss to competitors? Could it be that the prospect opts for an internal solution? Or could it be that the potential customers did not later need any solution at all?

Average Deal Size: This is the magnanimity of deals being spot by sales representatives. If a company is seeing deals coming in below-average, it may be a sign of the salespersons opting for smaller, easier wins or they are giving too many discounts on the normal deals just to make the sales.

DQ Dependency:

There are ways by which a company's statutes can further influence workers' DQ. The company's legacy, Culture, and Support Systems have a direct impact on the DQ of a salesperson however a good sales person knows how to deliver against all the odds. The following are some basic tips to note about DQ dependency.

a) Unrealistic growth targets have a greater negative impact on the motivation of the sales team which increases stress on the sales team. Demotivated sales team under stress push the sales team into the *Hyper DQ zone*. Some sales guys might even decide not to start in this direction end up in *Poor or Low DQ zone*.

b) If the companies don't have good people manager to motivate the sales team and develop a good team culture, the sales team under such influence moves into *Hyper DQ zone*. Poor team management and poor culture could also send some people into *Poor or Low DQ Zone*.

c) The support systems such as HR, Finance and Commercial teams of the organization could increase or decrease the DQ level of the sales teams.

This particular chapter has been stocked with ways to measure an individual's Dependency Quotient level both generally and in terms of sales. The chapter started out by discussing the general measurement of the Dependency Quotient. Furthermore the chapter discussed 5 major parameters for calculating a salesperson's DQ. Lastly, to top the cake with some icing, the chapter concluded by adding other ways by which employee's DQ is affected by the nature of the work and that is discussed in a sub-topic titled as the DQ dependencies. The next and final chapter discusses the Desperation Quotient Analysis which will give readers the essential tool sets that will make both salespersons and their employers get the best of each other for the attainment of departmental goals.

Chapter Five

Desperation Quotient Analysis (DQA)

We are now onto the concluding chapter of this book. The book started out by explaining the meaning of Desperation quotient by highlighting the relationship between capabilities and efforts as a marker for optimum desperation which is necessary for the best sales returns of any salesperson. Next, the book addressed the DQ graph that showed the four zones of DQ – the low, poor, hyper, and optimum DQ zones. Optimum DQ is identifiably the best zone as it combines efforts and capabilities to achieve. It is also known as the Perfect Desperation Quotient.

Perfect DQ is as good as a perfect Golf swing; no short-cuts. So, it's going to take a lot of discipline, hard work and focus to reach Optimum DQ. You can't blame anyone but yourself in the game of Golf. Similarly, once you decide to take a swing at 'sales' you are on your own. So, you better make sure you got all the practice you need, all the tools you need and you got a very good idea about the field.

DQ of a salesperson can be improved by systematic evaluation, enablement, execution, monitoring and continuous coaching. Over a period of time, your sales teams may have mastered the mistakes, which need to be corrected through the following process. Through the DQA process, we can make sure the salesperson understands which DQ Zone he is in. Depending on the DQ Zones, analyze the dependencies the person has to achieve their goals. Monitoring is a very important aspect of the DQA process after training.

Below is a chart of all necessary things to possess to reach a perfect DQ.

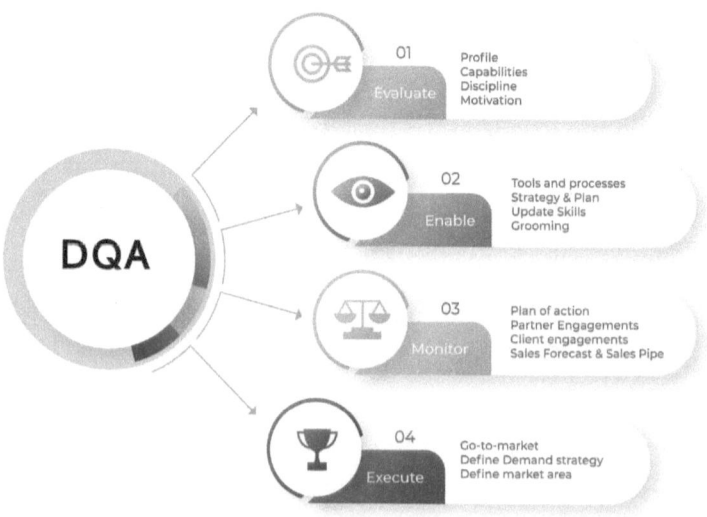

Evaluation includes assessing the profile of the sales person to identify the DQ Zone, reveal the current situation and plan to overcome it as required. To know that a disciplined sales person is must, despite the knowledge and hard work if the person is not disciplined enough, that person can't deliver consistently. To check motivation level is not easy, you will typically know this once the person starts moving in the market. However, managers can try to understand this by checking their preparation levels to start with. There are unique styles of sales approach, if one wants to operate solo, others may like a team around to support and motivate. Managers must understand and create the required environment to perform.

Enablement is a key function of a manager. It's not a good idea to wait until the salesperson makes mistakes or fails to achieve their targets. One must understand the enablement requirements in terms of knowledge, job skills, soft skills, competition, market, etc. Enablement of sales process is extremely important irrespective style and experiences one might have. Enablement must make the sales person aware of basic compliance and disciplinary needs of the brand. Ignorance of this key aspect may drown the person completely, at the worst case the brand.

Execution is ultimate part of this profession, this is the fun part. After all the preparation and enablement, ultimate outcome is a 'deal closed'. Ensure the sales team is making enough customer calls and the customers are actually interested in talking to your team. You have to find a way to analyse a successful customer call so that you know you are not losing your customers. While it is important that your team is talking to the customers, it's a need to talk to your strategic partners including your internal marketing team. You can't do it alone, you have to work as a team with your partners, learn to strike a balance here. While your team is generating leads, developing pipe and closing the gap with the deal closures, sales manager must ensure the win strategy is right, everyone in the organization is aligned to close a profitable deal. If you don't carry out strategies to win, you may not get the right deal.

Monitoring is a very important stage in this analysis. Monitoring refers to the organized procedure of collecting, analyzing and using information to keep tab on your set out task. Once you have recorded a success in the other stages, it is important that you put out a monitoring procedure so that there can be continuity to ensure that the goal is achieved.

Conclusion

Desperation Quotient – the extent to which you want to wake up and chase your dreams or the extent to which you want to continue in your slumber. From the dawn of this book, one thing has been highlighted and that is the relationship between the concept and factors of efforts and capabilities. It was made clear that the two concepts are interwoven but yet mutually exclusive – a dichotomy of perspective which in the end, gave way to the conclusion that to be able to harness the true power of self, the two must operate well simultaneously. The book went further to give the conceptual clarification of the term Desperation Quotient which is the ratio between the capabilities and the efforts that go into achieving personal and professional goals.

The Desperation Quotient could be shortened as DQ has four major zones which encapsulate every individual. Simply stating, an individual could either be an occupant of the low DQ zone, the poor DQ zone, the hyper DQ zone or be in the best zone which is the Optimum DQ Zone. The Optimum DQ Zone being the best is characterized with high capabilities and high level of efforts to further make the best of the capabilities. The chapter containing the zones also contained cases where the 4 zones are applicable so readers would be able to deduce what the scenario would most likely be for individual occupying each DQ zones. At this point, the book started leaning towards a direction where it had salespersons and the sales department as a focal point and so the readers were provided with a chapter on how to access the Optimum DQ zone as salespersons.

The remaining chapters talked explicitly on how to measure an individual's Desperation Quotient in general and as a salesperson in particular. The chapter also made mention of some DQ dependencies which could either help or mar the efforts of an employee. The last chapter of the book is an analysis of the DQ and in the chapter, there were guidelines for people to reach the best version of themselves in the career. The book has explained the concept of Desperation Quotient and by now readers must have been able to identify their respective DQ zones and ways by which they could level up by being the best version of themselves. Success does not come easily and there is only one corner of the universe you can be certain of improving and that is your own self. So why not start today right away? It is not as difficult as it seems all you need to do is to place yourself at the top of your to-do list every single day and the rest will fall into place.

Happy Selling!